THE PERSONAL
INTERNET
PASSWORD
ORGANIZER

A

WEB NAME:

WEB ADDRESS:

USERNAME:

PASSWORD:

NOTES:

WEB NAME:

WEB ADDRESS:

USERNAME:

PASSWORD:

NOTES:

WEB NAME:

WEB ADDRESS:

USERNAME:

PASSWORD:

NOTES:

WEB NAME:

WEB ADDRESS:

A

USERNAME:

PASSWORD:

NOTES:

WEB NAME:

WEB ADDRESS:

USERNAME:

PASSWORD:

NOTES:

WEB NAME:

WEB ADDRESS:

USERNAME:

PASSWORD:

NOTES:

A

WEB NAME:

WEB ADDRESS:

USERNAME:

PASSWORD:

NOTES:

WEB NAME:

WEB ADDRESS:

USERNAME:

PASSWORD:

NOTES:

WEB NAME:

WEB ADDRESS:

USERNAME:

PASSWORD:

NOTES:

WEB NAME:

WEB ADDRESS: A

USERNAME:

PASSWORD:

NOTES:

WEB NAME:

WEB ADDRESS:

USERNAME:

PASSWORD:

NOTES:

WEB NAME:

WEB ADDRESS:

USERNAME:

PASSWORD:

NOTES:

A

WEB NAME: _____

WEB ADDRESS: _____

USERNAME: _____

PASSWORD: _____

NOTES: _____

_____

_____

WEB NAME: _____

WEB ADDRESS: _____

USERNAME: _____

PASSWORD: _____

NOTES: _____

_____

_____

WEB NAME: _____

WEB ADDRESS: _____

USERNAME: _____

PASSWORD: _____

NOTES: _____

_____

_____

WEB NAME: _____

WEB ADDRESS: _____ A

USERNAME: _____

PASSWORD: _____

NOTES: _____

_____

_____

WEB NAME: _____

WEB ADDRESS: _____

USERNAME: _____

PASSWORD: _____

NOTES: _____

_____

_____

WEB NAME: _____

WEB ADDRESS: _____

USERNAME: _____

PASSWORD: _____

NOTES: _____

_____

_____

WEB NAME:

WEB ADDRESS:

B **USERNAME:**

PASSWORD:

NOTES:

WEB NAME:

WEB ADDRESS:

USERNAME:

PASSWORD:

NOTES:

WEB NAME:

WEB ADDRESS:

USERNAME:

PASSWORD:

NOTES:

WEB NAME:

WEB ADDRESS:

USERNAME: *B*

PASSWORD:

NOTES:

WEB NAME:

WEB ADDRESS:

USERNAME:

PASSWORD:

NOTES:

WEB NAME:

WEB ADDRESS:

USERNAME:

PASSWORD:

NOTES:

WEB NAME: _____

WEB ADDRESS: _____

B **USERNAME:** _____

PASSWORD: _____

NOTES: _____

_____

_____

WEB NAME: _____

WEB ADDRESS: _____

USERNAME: _____

PASSWORD: _____

NOTES: _____

_____

_____

WEB NAME: _____

WEB ADDRESS: _____

USERNAME: _____

PASSWORD: _____

NOTES: _____

_____

_____

WEB NAME:

WEB ADDRESS:

USERNAME: *B*

PASSWORD:

NOTES:

WEB NAME:

WEB ADDRESS:

USERNAME:

PASSWORD:

NOTES:

WEB NAME:

WEB ADDRESS:

USERNAME:

PASSWORD:

NOTES:

B

WEB NAME:

WEB ADDRESS:

USERNAME:

PASSWORD:

NOTES:

WEB NAME:

WEB ADDRESS:

USERNAME:

PASSWORD:

NOTES:

WEB NAME:

WEB ADDRESS:

USERNAME:

PASSWORD:

NOTES:

WEB NAME:

WEB ADDRESS:

USERNAME:

B

PASSWORD:

NOTES:

WEB NAME:

WEB ADDRESS:

USERNAME:

PASSWORD:

NOTES:

WEB NAME:

WEB ADDRESS:

USERNAME:

PASSWORD:

NOTES:

WEB NAME: _____

WEB ADDRESS: _____

USERNAME: _____

PASSWORD: _____

NOTES: _____

_____

_____

WEB NAME: _____

WEB ADDRESS: _____

USERNAME: _____

PASSWORD: _____

NOTES: _____

_____

_____

WEB NAME: _____

WEB ADDRESS: _____

USERNAME: _____

PASSWORD: _____

NOTES: _____

_____

_____

WEB NAME:

WEB ADDRESS:

USERNAME:

PASSWORD:

NOTES:

WEB NAME:

WEB ADDRESS:

USERNAME:

PASSWORD:

NOTES:

WEB NAME:

WEB ADDRESS:

USERNAME:

PASSWORD:

NOTES:

WEB NAME:

WEB ADDRESS:

USERNAME:

PASSWORD:

NOTES:

WEB NAME:

WEB ADDRESS:

USERNAME:

PASSWORD:

NOTES:

WEB NAME:

WEB ADDRESS:

USERNAME:

PASSWORD:

NOTES:

WEB NAME:

WEB ADDRESS:

USERNAME:

PASSWORD:

NOTES:

WEB NAME:

WEB ADDRESS:

USERNAME:

PASSWORD:

NOTES:

WEB NAME:

WEB ADDRESS:

USERNAME:

PASSWORD:

NOTES:

WEB NAME: _____

WEB ADDRESS: _____

USERNAME: _____

e **PASSWORD:** _____

NOTES: _____

_____

_____

WEB NAME: _____

WEB ADDRESS: _____

USERNAME: _____

PASSWORD: _____

NOTES: _____

_____

_____

WEB NAME: _____

WEB ADDRESS: _____

USERNAME: _____

PASSWORD: _____

NOTES: _____

_____

_____

WEB NAME: _____

WEB ADDRESS: _____

USERNAME: _____

PASSWORD: _____

NOTES: _____

_____

_____

WEB NAME: _____

WEB ADDRESS: _____

USERNAME: _____

PASSWORD: _____

NOTES: _____

_____

_____

WEB NAME: _____

WEB ADDRESS: _____

USERNAME: _____

PASSWORD: _____

NOTES: _____

_____

_____

WEB NAME:

WEB ADDRESS:

USERNAME:

PASSWORD:

D **NOTES:**

WEB NAME:

WEB ADDRESS:

USERNAME:

PASSWORD:

NOTES:

WEB NAME:

WEB ADDRESS:

USERNAME:

PASSWORD:

NOTES:

WEB NAME:

WEB ADDRESS:

USERNAME:

PASSWORD:

NOTES:

D

WEB NAME:

WEB ADDRESS:

USERNAME:

PASSWORD:

NOTES:

WEB NAME:

WEB ADDRESS:

USERNAME:

PASSWORD:

NOTES:

WEB NAME: _____

WEB ADDRESS: _____

USERNAME: _____

PASSWORD: _____

D **NOTES:** _____

_____

_____

WEB NAME: _____

WEB ADDRESS: _____

USERNAME: _____

PASSWORD: _____

NOTES: _____

_____

_____

WEB NAME: _____

WEB ADDRESS: _____

USERNAME: _____

PASSWORD: _____

NOTES: _____

_____

_____

WEB NAME:

WEB ADDRESS:

USERNAME:

PASSWORD:

NOTES:

D

WEB NAME:

WEB ADDRESS:

USERNAME:

PASSWORD:

NOTES:

WEB NAME:

WEB ADDRESS:

USERNAME:

PASSWORD:

NOTES:

WEB NAME:

WEB ADDRESS:

USERNAME:

PASSWORD:

D **NOTES:**

WEB NAME:

WEB ADDRESS:

USERNAME:

PASSWORD:

NOTES:

WEB NAME:

WEB ADDRESS:

USERNAME:

PASSWORD:

NOTES:

WEB NAME:

WEB ADDRESS:

USERNAME:

PASSWORD:

NOTES: *D*

WEB NAME:

WEB ADDRESS:

USERNAME:

PASSWORD:

NOTES:

WEB NAME:

WEB ADDRESS:

USERNAME:

PASSWORD:

NOTES:

WEB NAME:

WEB ADDRESS:

USERNAME:

PASSWORD:

NOTES:

WEB NAME:

WEB ADDRESS:

USERNAME:

PASSWORD:

NOTES:

WEB NAME:

WEB ADDRESS:

USERNAME:

PASSWORD:

NOTES:

WEB NAME:

WEB ADDRESS:

USERNAME:

PASSWORD:

NOTES:

WEB NAME:

WEB ADDRESS:

USERNAME:

PASSWORD:

NOTES:

WEB NAME:

WEB ADDRESS:

USERNAME:

PASSWORD:

NOTES:

WEB NAME:

WEB ADDRESS:

USERNAME:

PASSWORD:

NOTES:

e

WEB NAME:

WEB ADDRESS:

USERNAME:

PASSWORD:

NOTES:

WEB NAME:

WEB ADDRESS:

USERNAME:

PASSWORD:

NOTES:

WEB NAME:

WEB ADDRESS:

USERNAME:

PASSWORD:

NOTES:

WEB NAME:

WEB ADDRESS:

USERNAME:

PASSWORD:

NOTES:

WEB NAME:

WEB ADDRESS:

USERNAME:

PASSWORD:

NOTES:

WEB NAME: _____

WEB ADDRESS: _____

USERNAME: _____

PASSWORD: _____

NOTES: _____

_____

_____

WEB NAME: _____

WEB ADDRESS: _____

USERNAME: _____

PASSWORD: _____

NOTES: _____

_____

_____

WEB NAME: _____

WEB ADDRESS: _____

USERNAME: _____

PASSWORD: _____

NOTES: _____

_____

_____

WEB NAME: _____

WEB ADDRESS: _____

USERNAME: _____

PASSWORD: _____

NOTES: _____

_____

WEB NAME: _____

WEB ADDRESS: _____

USERNAME: _____

PASSWORD: _____

NOTES: _____

_____

WEB NAME: _____

WEB ADDRESS: _____

USERNAME: _____

PASSWORD: _____

NOTES: _____

_____

WEB NAME:

WEB ADDRESS:

USERNAME:

PASSWORD:

NOTES:

WEB NAME:

WEB ADDRESS:

USERNAME:

PASSWORD:

NOTES:

WEB NAME:

WEB ADDRESS:

USERNAME:

PASSWORD:

NOTES:

WEB NAME:

WEB ADDRESS:

USERNAME:

PASSWORD:

NOTES:

WEB NAME:

WEB ADDRESS:

USERNAME:

PASSWORD:

NOTES:

WEB NAME:

WEB ADDRESS:

USERNAME:

PASSWORD:

NOTES:

WEB NAME:

WEB ADDRESS:

USERNAME:

PASSWORD:

NOTES:

WEB NAME:

WEB ADDRESS:

USERNAME:

PASSWORD:

NOTES:

WEB NAME:

WEB ADDRESS:

USERNAME:

PASSWORD:

NOTES:

WEB NAME:

WEB ADDRESS:

USERNAME:

PASSWORD:

NOTES:

WEB NAME:

WEB ADDRESS:

USERNAME:

PASSWORD:

NOTES:

WEB NAME:

WEB ADDRESS:

USERNAME:

PASSWORD:

NOTES:

WEB NAME:

WEB ADDRESS:

USERNAME:

PASSWORD:

NOTES:

WEB NAME:

WEB ADDRESS:

USERNAME:

PASSWORD:

NOTES:

WEB NAME:

WEB ADDRESS:

USERNAME:

PASSWORD:

NOTES:

WEB NAME:

WEB ADDRESS:

USERNAME:

PASSWORD:

NOTES:

WEB NAME: *G*

WEB ADDRESS:

USERNAME:

PASSWORD:

NOTES:

WEB NAME:

WEB ADDRESS:

USERNAME:

PASSWORD:

NOTES:

WEB NAME: _____

WEB ADDRESS: _____

USERNAME: _____

PASSWORD: _____

NOTES: _____

_____

WEB NAME: _____

WEB ADDRESS: _____

USERNAME: _____

PASSWORD: _____

NOTES: _____

_____

WEB NAME: _____

WEB ADDRESS: _____

USERNAME: _____

PASSWORD: _____

NOTES: _____

_____

_____

WEB NAME:

WEB ADDRESS:

USERNAME:

PASSWORD:

NOTES:

WEB NAME:

WEB ADDRESS:

USERNAME:

PASSWORD:

NOTES:

WEB NAME:

WEB ADDRESS:

USERNAME:

PASSWORD:

NOTES:

WEB NAME: _____

WEB ADDRESS: _____

USERNAME: _____

PASSWORD: _____

NOTES: _____

_____

_____

_G_ **WEB NAME:** _____

WEB ADDRESS: _____

USERNAME: _____

PASSWORD: _____

NOTES: _____

_____

_____

WEB NAME: _____

WEB ADDRESS: _____

USERNAME: _____

PASSWORD: _____

NOTES: _____

_____

_____

WEB NAME: _____

WEB ADDRESS: _____

USERNAME: _____

PASSWORD: _____

NOTES: _____

_____

WEB NAME: _____ *G*

WEB ADDRESS: _____

USERNAME: _____

PASSWORD: _____

NOTES: _____

_____

WEB NAME: _____

WEB ADDRESS: _____

USERNAME: _____

PASSWORD: _____

NOTES: _____

_____

WEB NAME: _____

WEB ADDRESS: _____

USERNAME: _____

PASSWORD: _____

NOTES: _____

_____

_____

WEB NAME: _____

WEB ADDRESS: _____

USERNAME: _____

PASSWORD: _____

NOTES: _____

_____

_____

WEB NAME: _____

WEB ADDRESS: _____

USERNAME: _____

PASSWORD: _____

NOTES: _____

_____

_____

WEB NAME:

WEB ADDRESS:

USERNAME:

PASSWORD:

NOTES:

WEB NAME:

WEB ADDRESS:

USERNAME:

PASSWORD:

NOTES:

WEB NAME:

WEB ADDRESS:

USERNAME:

PASSWORD:

NOTES:

WEB NAME:

WEB ADDRESS:

USERNAME:

PASSWORD:

NOTES:

WEB NAME:

WEB ADDRESS:

USERNAME:

PASSWORD:

NOTES:

WEB NAME:

WEB ADDRESS:

USERNAME:

PASSWORD:

NOTES:

WEB NAME: _____

WEB ADDRESS: _____

USERNAME: _____

PASSWORD: _____

NOTES: _____

_____

_____

WEB NAME: _____

WEB ADDRESS: _____

USERNAME: _____

PASSWORD: _____

NOTES: _____

_____

_____

WEB NAME: _____

WEB ADDRESS: _____

USERNAME: _____

PASSWORD: _____

NOTES: _____

_____

_____

WEB NAME: _____

WEB ADDRESS: _____

USERNAME: _____

PASSWORD: _____

NOTES: _____

_____

_____

WEB NAME: _____

WEB ADDRESS: _____

USERNAME: _____

PASSWORD: _____

NOTES: _____

_____

_____

WEB NAME: _____

WEB ADDRESS: _____

USERNAME: _____

PASSWORD: _____

NOTES: _____

_____

_____

WEB NAME:

WEB ADDRESS:

USERNAME:

PASSWORD:

NOTES:

WEB NAME:

WEB ADDRESS:

USERNAME:

PASSWORD:

NOTES:

WEB NAME:

WEB ADDRESS:

USERNAME:

PASSWORD:

NOTES:

WEB NAME:

WEB ADDRESS:

USERNAME:

PASSWORD:

NOTES:

WEB NAME:

WEB ADDRESS:

J **USERNAME:**

PASSWORD:

NOTES:

WEB NAME:

WEB ADDRESS:

USERNAME:

PASSWORD:

NOTES:

WEB NAME: _____

WEB ADDRESS: _____

USERNAME: _____

PASSWORD: _____

NOTES: _____

_____

_____

WEB NAME: _____

WEB ADDRESS: _____

USERNAME: _____

PASSWORD: _____

NOTES: _____

_____

_____

WEB NAME: _____

WEB ADDRESS: _____

USERNAME: _____

PASSWORD: _____

NOTES: _____

_____

_____

WEB NAME:

WEB ADDRESS:

USERNAME:

PASSWORD:

NOTES:

WEB NAME:

WEB ADDRESS:

J **USERNAME:**

PASSWORD:

NOTES:

WEB NAME:

WEB ADDRESS:

USERNAME:

PASSWORD:

NOTES:

WEB NAME:

WEB ADDRESS:

USERNAME:

PASSWORD:

NOTES:

WEB NAME:

WEB ADDRESS:

USERNAME:

PASSWORD:

NOTES:

WEB NAME:

WEB ADDRESS:

USERNAME:

PASSWORD:

NOTES:

WEB NAME:

WEB ADDRESS:

USERNAME:

PASSWORD:

NOTES:

WEB NAME:

WEB ADDRESS:

J **USERNAME:**

PASSWORD:

NOTES:

WEB NAME:

WEB ADDRESS:

USERNAME:

PASSWORD:

NOTES:

WEB NAME:

WEB ADDRESS:

USERNAME:

PASSWORD:

NOTES:

WEB NAME:

WEB ADDRESS:

USERNAME:

PASSWORD:

NOTES:

WEB NAME:

WEB ADDRESS:

USERNAME:

PASSWORD:

NOTES:

WEB NAME:

WEB ADDRESS:

USERNAME:

PASSWORD:

NOTES:

WEB NAME:

WEB ADDRESS:

USERNAME:

J **PASSWORD:**

NOTES:

WEB NAME:

WEB ADDRESS:

USERNAME:

PASSWORD:

NOTES:

WEB NAME:

WEB ADDRESS:

USERNAME:

PASSWORD:

NOTES:

WEB NAME:

WEB ADDRESS:

USERNAME:

PASSWORD:

NOTES:

WEB NAME:

WEB ADDRESS:

USERNAME:

PASSWORD:

NOTES:

WEB NAME:

WEB ADDRESS:

USERNAME:

PASSWORD:

NOTES:

WEB NAME:

WEB ADDRESS:

USERNAME:

J **PASSWORD:**

NOTES:

WEB NAME:

WEB ADDRESS:

USERNAME:

PASSWORD:

NOTES:

WEB NAME:

WEB ADDRESS:

USERNAME:

PASSWORD:

NOTES:

WEB NAME:

WEB ADDRESS:

USERNAME:

PASSWORD:

NOTES:

WEB NAME:

WEB ADDRESS:

USERNAME:

PASSWORD:

NOTES:

WEB NAME:

WEB ADDRESS:

USERNAME:

PASSWORD:

NOTES:

WEB NAME:

WEB ADDRESS:

USERNAME:

J **PASSWORD:**

NOTES:

WEB NAME:

WEB ADDRESS:

USERNAME:

PASSWORD:

NOTES:

WEB NAME:

WEB ADDRESS:

USERNAME:

PASSWORD:

NOTES:

WEB NAME:

WEB ADDRESS:

USERNAME:

PASSWORD: **J**

NOTES:

WEB NAME:

WEB ADDRESS:

USERNAME:

PASSWORD:

NOTES:

WEB NAME:

WEB ADDRESS:

USERNAME:

PASSWORD:

NOTES:

WEB NAME:

WEB ADDRESS:

USERNAME:

PASSWORD:

NOTES:

WEB NAME:

WEB ADDRESS:

USERNAME:

PASSWORD:

NOTES:

WEB NAME: _____

WEB ADDRESS: _____

USERNAME: _____

PASSWORD: _____

NOTES: _____

_____

_____

WEB NAME: _____

WEB ADDRESS: _____

USERNAME: _____

PASSWORD: _____

NOTES: _____

_____

_____

WEB NAME: _____

WEB ADDRESS: _____

USERNAME: _____

PASSWORD: _____

NOTES: _____

_____

_____

WEB NAME: _____

WEB ADDRESS: _____

USERNAME: _____

PASSWORD: _____

NOTES: _____

_____

_____

WEB NAME: _____

WEB ADDRESS: _____

USERNAME: _____

PASSWORD: _____

NOTES: _____

_____

_____

WEB NAME: _____

WEB ADDRESS: _____

USERNAME: _____

PASSWORD: _____

NOTES: _____

_____

_____

WEB NAME:

WEB ADDRESS:

USERNAME:

PASSWORD:

NOTES:

WEB NAME:

WEB ADDRESS:

USERNAME:

PASSWORD:

NOTES:

WEB NAME:

WEB ADDRESS:

USERNAME:

PASSWORD:

NOTES:

WEB NAME:

WEB ADDRESS:

USERNAME:

PASSWORD:

NOTES:

WEB NAME:

WEB ADDRESS:

USERNAME:

PASSWORD:

NOTES:

WEB NAME:

WEB ADDRESS:

USERNAME:

PASSWORD:

NOTES:

WEB NAME:

WEB ADDRESS:

USERNAME:

PASSWORD:

NOTES:

WEB NAME:

WEB ADDRESS:

USERNAME:

PASSWORD:

NOTES:

WEB NAME:

WEB ADDRESS:

USERNAME:

PASSWORD:

NOTES:

WEB NAME: _____

WEB ADDRESS: _____

USERNAME: _____

PASSWORD: _____

NOTES: _____

_____

_____

WEB NAME: _____

WEB ADDRESS: _____

USERNAME: _____

PASSWORD: _____

NOTES: _____

_____

_____

WEB NAME: _____

WEB ADDRESS: _____

USERNAME: _____

PASSWORD: _____

NOTES: _____

_____

_____

WEB NAME:

WEB ADDRESS:

USERNAME:

PASSWORD:

NOTES:

WEB NAME:

WEB ADDRESS:

USERNAME:

PASSWORD:

NOTES:

WEB NAME:

WEB ADDRESS:

USERNAME:

PASSWORD:

NOTES:

WEB NAME:

WEB ADDRESS:

USERNAME:

PASSWORD:

NOTES:

WEB NAME:

WEB ADDRESS:

USERNAME:

PASSWORD:

NOTES:

L

WEB NAME:

WEB ADDRESS:

USERNAME:

PASSWORD:

NOTES:

WEB NAME:

WEB ADDRESS:

USERNAME:

PASSWORD:

NOTES:

WEB NAME:

WEB ADDRESS:

USERNAME:

PASSWORD:

NOTES:

WEB NAME:

WEB ADDRESS:

USERNAME:

PASSWORD:

NOTES:

WEB NAME:

WEB ADDRESS:

USERNAME:

PASSWORD:

NOTES:

WEB NAME:

WEB ADDRESS:

USERNAME:

PASSWORD:

NOTES:

WEB NAME:

WEB ADDRESS:

USERNAME:

PASSWORD:

NOTES:

WEB NAME:

WEB ADDRESS:

USERNAME:

PASSWORD:

NOTES:

WEB NAME:

WEB ADDRESS:

USERNAME:

PASSWORD:

NOTES:

WEB NAME:

WEB ADDRESS:

USERNAME:

PASSWORD:

NOTES:

WEB NAME:

WEB ADDRESS:

USERNAME:

PASSWORD:

NOTES:

WEB NAME:

WEB ADDRESS:

USERNAME:

PASSWORD:

NOTES:

M

WEB NAME:

WEB ADDRESS:

USERNAME:

PASSWORD:

NOTES:

WEB NAME:

WEB ADDRESS:

USERNAME:

PASSWORD:

NOTES:

WEB NAME:

WEB ADDRESS:

USERNAME:

PASSWORD:

NOTES:

M

WEB NAME:

WEB ADDRESS:

USERNAME:

PASSWORD:

NOTES:

WEB NAME:

WEB ADDRESS:

USERNAME:

PASSWORD:

NOTES:

WEB NAME:

WEB ADDRESS:

USERNAME:

PASSWORD:

NOTES:

M

WEB NAME:

WEB ADDRESS:

USERNAME:

PASSWORD:

NOTES:

WEB NAME: _____

WEB ADDRESS: _____

USERNAME: _____

PASSWORD: _____

NOTES: _____

_____

_____

WEB NAME: _____

WEB ADDRESS: _____

USERNAME: _____

PASSWORD: _____

NOTES: _____

_____

_____

WEB NAME: _____

WEB ADDRESS: _____

USERNAME: _____

PASSWORD: _____

NOTES: _____

_____

_____

WEB NAME: _____

WEB ADDRESS: _____

USERNAME: _____

PASSWORD: _____

NOTES: _____

_____

_____

WEB NAME: _____

WEB ADDRESS: _____

USERNAME: _____

PASSWORD: _____

NOTES: _____

M _____

_____

WEB NAME: _____

WEB ADDRESS: _____

USERNAME: _____

PASSWORD: _____

NOTES: _____

_____

_____

WEB NAME:

WEB ADDRESS:

USERNAME:

PASSWORD:

NOTES:

WEB NAME:

WEB ADDRESS:

USERNAME:

PASSWORD:

NOTES:

WEB NAME:

WEB ADDRESS:

USERNAME:

PASSWORD:

NOTES:

WEB NAME: _____

WEB ADDRESS: _____

USERNAME: _____

PASSWORD: _____

NOTES: _____

_____

_____

WEB NAME: _____

WEB ADDRESS: _____

USERNAME: _____

PASSWORD: _____

NOTES: _____

_____

_____

N **WEB NAME:** _____

WEB ADDRESS: _____

USERNAME: _____

PASSWORD: _____

NOTES: _____

_____

_____

WEB NAME:

WEB ADDRESS:

USERNAME:

PASSWORD:

NOTES:

WEB NAME:

WEB ADDRESS:

USERNAME:

PASSWORD:

NOTES:

WEB NAME: *N*

WEB ADDRESS:

USERNAME:

PASSWORD:

NOTES:

WEB NAME:

WEB ADDRESS:

USERNAME:

PASSWORD:

NOTES:

WEB NAME:

WEB ADDRESS:

USERNAME:

PASSWORD:

NOTES:

N **WEB NAME:**

WEB ADDRESS:

USERNAME:

PASSWORD:

NOTES:

WEB NAME:

WEB ADDRESS:

USERNAME:

PASSWORD:

NOTES:

WEB NAME:

WEB ADDRESS:

USERNAME:

PASSWORD:

NOTES:

WEB NAME: *N*

WEB ADDRESS:

USERNAME:

PASSWORD:

NOTES:

WEB NAME: _____

WEB ADDRESS: _____

USERNAME: _____

PASSWORD: _____

NOTES: _____

_____

_____

WEB NAME: _____

WEB ADDRESS: _____

USERNAME: _____

PASSWORD: _____

NOTES: _____

_____

_____

N **WEB NAME:** _____

WEB ADDRESS: _____

USERNAME: _____

PASSWORD: _____

NOTES: _____

_____

_____

WEB NAME:

WEB ADDRESS:

USERNAME:

PASSWORD:

NOTES:

WEB NAME:

WEB ADDRESS:

USERNAME:

PASSWORD:

NOTES:

WEB NAME:

WEB ADDRESS:

USERNAME:

PASSWORD:

NOTES:

WEB NAME: _____

WEB ADDRESS: _____

USERNAME: _____

PASSWORD: _____

NOTES: _____

_____

_____

WEB NAME: _____

WEB ADDRESS: _____

USERNAME: _____

PASSWORD: _____

NOTES: _____

_____

_____

WEB NAME: _____

WEB ADDRESS: _____

USERNAME: _____

PASSWORD: _____

NOTES: _____

_____

_____

WEB NAME:

WEB ADDRESS:

USERNAME:

PASSWORD:

NOTES:

WEB NAME:

WEB ADDRESS:

USERNAME:

PASSWORD:

NOTES:

WEB NAME:

WEB ADDRESS:

USERNAME:

PASSWORD:

NOTES:

WEB NAME:

WEB ADDRESS:

USERNAME:

PASSWORD:

NOTES:

WEB NAME:

WEB ADDRESS:

USERNAME:

PASSWORD:

NOTES:

WEB NAME:

WEB ADDRESS:

USERNAME:

PASSWORD:

NOTES:

WEB NAME:

WEB ADDRESS:

USERNAME:

PASSWORD:

NOTES:

WEB NAME:

WEB ADDRESS:

USERNAME:

PASSWORD:

NOTES:

WEB NAME:

WEB ADDRESS:

USERNAME:

PASSWORD:

NOTES:

WEB NAME:

WEB ADDRESS:

USERNAME:

PASSWORD:

NOTES:

WEB NAME:

WEB ADDRESS:

USERNAME:

PASSWORD:

NOTES:

WEB NAME:

WEB ADDRESS:

USERNAME:

PASSWORD:

NOTES:

WEB NAME:

WEB ADDRESS:

USERNAME:

PASSWORD:

NOTES:

WEB NAME:

WEB ADDRESS:

USERNAME:

PASSWORD:

NOTES:

WEB NAME:

WEB ADDRESS:

USERNAME:

PASSWORD:

NOTES:

WEB NAME:

WEB ADDRESS:

USERNAME:

PASSWORD:

NOTES:

WEB NAME:

WEB ADDRESS:

USERNAME:

PASSWORD:

NOTES:

WEB NAME:

WEB ADDRESS:

USERNAME:

PASSWORD:

NOTES:

WEB NAME:

WEB ADDRESS:

USERNAME:

PASSWORD:

NOTES:

WEB NAME:

WEB ADDRESS:

USERNAME:

PASSWORD:

NOTES:

WEB NAME:

WEB ADDRESS:

USERNAME:

PASSWORD:

NOTES:

WEB NAME:

WEB ADDRESS:

USERNAME:

PASSWORD:

NOTES:

WEB NAME:

WEB ADDRESS:

USERNAME:

PASSWORD:

NOTES:

WEB NAME:

WEB ADDRESS:

USERNAME:

PASSWORD:

NOTES:

WEB NAME:

WEB ADDRESS:

USERNAME:

PASSWORD:

NOTES:

WEB NAME:

WEB ADDRESS:

USERNAME:

PASSWORD:

NOTES:

WEB NAME:

WEB ADDRESS:

USERNAME:

PASSWORD:

NOTES:

WEB NAME:

WEB ADDRESS:

USERNAME:

PASSWORD:

NOTES:

WEB NAME:

WEB ADDRESS:

USERNAME:

PASSWORD:

NOTES:

WEB NAME:

WEB ADDRESS:

USERNAME:

PASSWORD:

NOTES:

WEB NAME:

WEB ADDRESS:

USERNAME:

PASSWORD:

NOTES:

WEB NAME:

WEB ADDRESS:

USERNAME:

PASSWORD:

NOTES:

WEB NAME:

WEB ADDRESS:

USERNAME:

PASSWORD:

NOTES:

WEB NAME: _____

WEB ADDRESS: _____

USERNAME: _____

PASSWORD: _____

NOTES: _____

_____

WEB NAME: _____

WEB ADDRESS: _____

USERNAME: _____

PASSWORD: _____

NOTES: _____

_____

WEB NAME: _____

WEB ADDRESS: _____

USERNAME: _____

PASSWORD: _____

NOTES: _____

_____

WEB NAME:

WEB ADDRESS:

USERNAME:

PASSWORD:

NOTES:

WEB NAME:

WEB ADDRESS:

USERNAME:

PASSWORD:

NOTES:

WEB NAME:

WEB ADDRESS:

USERNAME:

PASSWORD:

NOTES:

WEB NAME:

WEB ADDRESS:

USERNAME:

PASSWORD:

NOTES:

WEB NAME:

WEB ADDRESS:

USERNAME:

PASSWORD:

NOTES:

WEB NAME:

WEB ADDRESS:

USERNAME:

PASSWORD:

NOTES:

WEB NAME:

WEB ADDRESS:

USERNAME:

PASSWORD:

NOTES:

WEB NAME:

WEB ADDRESS:

USERNAME:

PASSWORD:

NOTES:

WEB NAME:

WEB ADDRESS:

USERNAME:

PASSWORD:

NOTES:

WEB NAME: _____

WEB ADDRESS: _____

USERNAME: _____

PASSWORD: _____

NOTES: _____

_____

_____

WEB NAME: _____

WEB ADDRESS: _____

USERNAME: _____

PASSWORD: _____

NOTES: _____

_____

_____

WEB NAME: _____

WEB ADDRESS: _____

USERNAME: _____

PASSWORD: _____

NOTES: _____

_____

_____

WEB NAME:

WEB ADDRESS:

USERNAME:

PASSWORD:

NOTES:

WEB NAME:

WEB ADDRESS:

USERNAME:

PASSWORD:

NOTES:

WEB NAME:

WEB ADDRESS:

USERNAME:

PASSWORD:

Q

NOTES:

WEB NAME:

WEB ADDRESS:

USERNAME:

PASSWORD:

NOTES:

WEB NAME:

WEB ADDRESS:

USERNAME:

PASSWORD:

NOTES:

WEB NAME:

WEB ADDRESS:

USERNAME:

PASSWORD:

NOTES:

WEB NAME: _____

WEB ADDRESS: _____

USERNAME: _____

PASSWORD: _____

NOTES: _____

_____

_____

WEB NAME: _____

WEB ADDRESS: _____

USERNAME: _____

PASSWORD: _____

NOTES: _____

_____

_____

WEB NAME: _____

WEB ADDRESS: _____

USERNAME: _____

PASSWORD: _____ Q

NOTES: _____

_____

_____

WEB NAME:

WEB ADDRESS:

USERNAME:

PASSWORD:

NOTES:

WEB NAME:

WEB ADDRESS:

USERNAME:

PASSWORD:

NOTES:

WEB NAME:

WEB ADDRESS:

USERNAME:

PASSWORD:

NOTES:

WEB NAME: _____

WEB ADDRESS: _____

USERNAME: _____

PASSWORD: _____

NOTES: _____

_____

_____

WEB NAME: _____

WEB ADDRESS: _____

USERNAME: _____

PASSWORD: _____

NOTES: _____

_____

_____

WEB NAME: _____

WEB ADDRESS: _____

USERNAME: _____

PASSWORD: _____

NOTES: _____

_____

_____

WEB NAME:

WEB ADDRESS:

USERNAME:

PASSWORD:

NOTES:

WEB NAME:

WEB ADDRESS:

USERNAME:

PASSWORD:

NOTES:

WEB NAME:

WEB ADDRESS:

USERNAME:

PASSWORD:

NOTES:

WEB NAME: _____

WEB ADDRESS: _____

USERNAME: _____

PASSWORD: _____

NOTES: _____

_____

_____

WEB NAME: _____

WEB ADDRESS: _____

USERNAME: _____

PASSWORD: _____

NOTES: _____

_____

_____

WEB NAME: _____

WEB ADDRESS: _____

USERNAME: _____

PASSWORD: _____

NOTES: _____

_____

_____

WEB NAME:

WEB ADDRESS:

USERNAME:

PASSWORD:

NOTES:

WEB NAME:

WEB ADDRESS:

USERNAME:

PASSWORD:

NOTES:

WEB NAME:

WEB ADDRESS:

USERNAME:

PASSWORD:

NOTES:

WEB NAME:

WEB ADDRESS:

USERNAME:

PASSWORD:

NOTES:

WEB NAME:

WEB ADDRESS:

USERNAME:

PASSWORD:

NOTES:

WEB NAME:

WEB ADDRESS:

USERNAME:

PASSWORD:

NOTES:

WEB NAME:

WEB ADDRESS:

USERNAME:

PASSWORD:

NOTES:

WEB NAME:

WEB ADDRESS:

USERNAME:

PASSWORD:

NOTES:

WEB NAME:

S **WEB ADDRESS:**

USERNAME:

PASSWORD:

NOTES:

WEB NAME: _____

WEB ADDRESS: _____

USERNAME: _____

PASSWORD: _____

NOTES: _____

_____

_____

WEB NAME: _____

WEB ADDRESS: _____

USERNAME: _____

PASSWORD: _____

NOTES: _____

_____

_____

WEB NAME: _____

WEB ADDRESS: _____ S

USERNAME: _____

PASSWORD: _____

NOTES: _____

_____

_____

WEB NAME:

WEB ADDRESS:

USERNAME:

PASSWORD:

NOTES:

WEB NAME:

WEB ADDRESS:

USERNAME:

PASSWORD:

NOTES:

WEB NAME:

WEB ADDRESS:

USERNAME:

PASSWORD:

NOTES:

WEB NAME:

WEB ADDRESS:

USERNAME:

PASSWORD:

NOTES:

WEB NAME:

WEB ADDRESS:

USERNAME:

PASSWORD:

NOTES:

WEB NAME:

WEB ADDRESS:

USERNAME:

PASSWORD:

NOTES:

WEB NAME: _____

WEB ADDRESS: _____

USERNAME: _____

PASSWORD: _____

NOTES: _____

_____

_____

WEB NAME: _____

WEB ADDRESS: _____

USERNAME: _____

PASSWORD: _____

NOTES: _____

_____

_____

WEB NAME: _____

S **WEB ADDRESS:** _____

USERNAME: _____

PASSWORD: _____

NOTES: _____

_____

_____

WEB NAME:

WEB ADDRESS:

USERNAME:

PASSWORD:

NOTES:

WEB NAME:

WEB ADDRESS:

USERNAME:

PASSWORD:

NOTES:

WEB NAME:

WEB ADDRESS:

USERNAME:

PASSWORD:

NOTES:

WEB NAME:

WEB ADDRESS:

USERNAME:

PASSWORD:

NOTES:

WEB NAME:

WEB ADDRESS:

USERNAME:

PASSWORD:

NOTES:

WEB NAME:

WEB ADDRESS:

USERNAME:

PASSWORD:

NOTES:

WEB NAME:

WEB ADDRESS:

USERNAME:

PASSWORD:

NOTES:

WEB NAME:

WEB ADDRESS:

USERNAME:

PASSWORD:

NOTES:

WEB NAME:

WEB ADDRESS:

USERNAME:

PASSWORD:

NOTES:

WEB NAME:

WEB ADDRESS:

USERNAME:

PASSWORD:

NOTES:

WEB NAME:

WEB ADDRESS:

USERNAME:

PASSWORD:

NOTES:

WEB NAME:

WEB ADDRESS:

USERNAME:

PASSWORD:

NOTES:

WEB NAME:

WEB ADDRESS:

USERNAME:

PASSWORD:

NOTES:

WEB NAME:

WEB ADDRESS:

USERNAME:

PASSWORD:

NOTES:

WEB NAME:

WEB ADDRESS:

USERNAME:

PASSWORD:

NOTES:

WEB NAME: _____

WEB ADDRESS: _____

USERNAME: _____

PASSWORD: _____

NOTES: _____

_____

_____

WEB NAME: _____

WEB ADDRESS: _____

USERNAME: _____

PASSWORD: _____

NOTES: _____

_____

_____

WEB NAME: _____

WEB ADDRESS: _____

USERNAME: _____

PASSWORD: _____

NOTES: _____

_____

_____

WEB NAME:

WEB ADDRESS:

USERNAME:

PASSWORD:

NOTES:

WEB NAME:

WEB ADDRESS:

USERNAME:

PASSWORD:

NOTES:

WEB NAME:

WEB ADDRESS:

USERNAME:

PASSWORD:

NOTES:

WEB NAME: _____

WEB ADDRESS: _____

USERNAME: _____

PASSWORD: _____

NOTES: _____

_____

_____

WEB NAME: _____

WEB ADDRESS: _____

USERNAME: _____

PASSWORD: _____

NOTES: _____

_____

_____

WEB NAME: _____

WEB ADDRESS: _____

USERNAME: _____

u **PASSWORD:** _____

NOTES: _____

_____

_____

WEB NAME:

WEB ADDRESS:

USERNAME:

PASSWORD:

NOTES:

WEB NAME:

WEB ADDRESS:

USERNAME:

PASSWORD:

NOTES:

WEB NAME:

WEB ADDRESS:

USERNAME:

PASSWORD:

NOTES:

WEB NAME: _____

WEB ADDRESS: _____

USERNAME: _____

PASSWORD: _____

NOTES: _____

_____

_____

WEB NAME: _____

WEB ADDRESS: _____

USERNAME: _____

PASSWORD: _____

NOTES: _____

_____

_____

WEB NAME: _____

WEB ADDRESS: _____

USERNAME: _____

PASSWORD: _____

NOTES: _____

_____

_____

WEB NAME: _____

WEB ADDRESS: _____

USERNAME: _____

PASSWORD: _____

NOTES: _____

_____

_____

WEB NAME: _____

WEB ADDRESS: _____

USERNAME: _____

PASSWORD: _____

NOTES: _____

_____

_____

WEB NAME: _____

WEB ADDRESS: _____

USERNAME: _____

PASSWORD: _____

NOTES: _____

_____

_____

WEB NAME:

WEB ADDRESS:

USERNAME:

PASSWORD:

NOTES:

WEB NAME:

WEB ADDRESS:

USERNAME:

PASSWORD:

NOTES:

WEB NAME:

WEB ADDRESS:

USERNAME:

PASSWORD:

NOTES:

WEB NAME:

WEB ADDRESS:

USERNAME:

PASSWORD:

NOTES:

WEB NAME:

WEB ADDRESS:

USERNAME:

PASSWORD:

NOTES:

WEB NAME:

WEB ADDRESS:

USERNAME:

PASSWORD:

u

NOTES:

WEB NAME:

WEB ADDRESS:

USERNAME:

PASSWORD:

NOTES:

WEB NAME:

WEB ADDRESS:

USERNAME:

PASSWORD:

NOTES:

WEB NAME:

WEB ADDRESS:

USERNAME:

PASSWORD:

NOTES:

WEB NAME:

WEB ADDRESS:

USERNAME:

PASSWORD:

NOTES:

WEB NAME:

WEB ADDRESS:

USERNAME:

PASSWORD:

NOTES:

WEB NAME:

WEB ADDRESS:

USERNAME:

PASSWORD:

NOTES:

WEB NAME:

WEB ADDRESS:

USERNAME:

PASSWORD:

NOTES:

WEB NAME:

WEB ADDRESS:

USERNAME:

PASSWORD:

NOTES:

WEB NAME:

WEB ADDRESS:

USERNAME:

PASSWORD:

NOTES:

WEB NAME:

WEB ADDRESS:

USERNAME:

PASSWORD:

NOTES:

WEB NAME:

WEB ADDRESS:

USERNAME:

PASSWORD:

NOTES:

WEB NAME:

WEB ADDRESS:

USERNAME:

PASSWORD:

NOTES:

WEB NAME: _____

WEB ADDRESS: _____

USERNAME: _____

PASSWORD: _____

NOTES: _____

_____

_____

WEB NAME: _____

WEB ADDRESS: _____

USERNAME: _____

PASSWORD: _____

NOTES: _____

_____

_____

WEB NAME: _____

WEB ADDRESS: _____

USERNAME: _____

PASSWORD: _____

NOTES: _____

_____

_____

WEB NAME:

WEB ADDRESS:

USERNAME:

PASSWORD:

NOTES:

WEB NAME:

WEB ADDRESS:

USERNAME:

PASSWORD:

NOTES:

WEB NAME:

WEB ADDRESS:

USERNAME:

PASSWORD:

NOTES:

WEB NAME:

WEB ADDRESS:

USERNAME:

PASSWORD:

NOTES:

WEB NAME:

WEB ADDRESS:

USERNAME:

PASSWORD:

NOTES:

WEB NAME:

WEB ADDRESS:

USERNAME:

PASSWORD:

NOTES:

WEB NAME: _____

WEB ADDRESS: _____

USERNAME: _____

PASSWORD: _____

NOTES: _____

_____

_____

WEB NAME: _____

WEB ADDRESS: _____

USERNAME: _____

PASSWORD: _____

NOTES: _____

_____

_____

WEB NAME: _____

WEB ADDRESS: _____

USERNAME: _____

PASSWORD: _____

NOTES: _____

_____

_____

WEB NAME:

WEB ADDRESS:

USERNAME:

PASSWORD:

NOTES:

WEB NAME:

WEB ADDRESS:

USERNAME:

PASSWORD:

NOTES:

WEB NAME:

WEB ADDRESS:

USERNAME:

PASSWORD:

NOTES:

WEB NAME:

WEB ADDRESS:

USERNAME:

PASSWORD:

NOTES:

WEB NAME:

WEB ADDRESS:

USERNAME:

PASSWORD:

NOTES:

WEB NAME:

WEB ADDRESS:

USERNAME:

PASSWORD:

NOTES:

WEB NAME:

WEB ADDRESS:

USERNAME:

PASSWORD:

NOTES:

WEB NAME:

WEB ADDRESS:

USERNAME:

PASSWORD:

NOTES:

WEB NAME:

WEB ADDRESS:

USERNAME:

PASSWORD:

NOTES:

WEB NAME:

WEB ADDRESS:

USERNAME:

PASSWORD:

NOTES:

WEB NAME:

WEB ADDRESS:

USERNAME:

PASSWORD:

NOTES:

WEB NAME:

WEB ADDRESS:

USERNAME:

PASSWORD:

NOTES:

WEB NAME:

WEB ADDRESS:

USERNAME:

PASSWORD:

NOTES:

WEB NAME:

WEB ADDRESS:

USERNAME:

PASSWORD:

NOTES:

WEB NAME:

WEB ADDRESS:

USERNAME:

PASSWORD:

NOTES:

X

WEB NAME:

WEB ADDRESS:

USERNAME:

PASSWORD:

NOTES:

WEB NAME:

WEB ADDRESS:

USERNAME:

PASSWORD:

NOTES:

WEB NAME:

WEB ADDRESS:

USERNAME:

PASSWORD:

NOTES:

X

WEB NAME:

WEB ADDRESS:

USERNAME:

PASSWORD:

NOTES:

WEB NAME:

WEB ADDRESS:

USERNAME:

PASSWORD:

NOTES:

WEB NAME:

WEB ADDRESS:

USERNAME:

PASSWORD:

NOTES:

X

WEB NAME:

WEB ADDRESS:

USERNAME:

PASSWORD:

NOTES:

WEB NAME:

WEB ADDRESS:

USERNAME:

PASSWORD:

NOTES:

WEB NAME:

WEB ADDRESS:

USERNAME:

PASSWORD:

NOTES:

X

WEB NAME:

WEB ADDRESS:

USERNAME:

PASSWORD:

NOTES:

WEB NAME:

WEB ADDRESS:

USERNAME:

PASSWORD:

NOTES:

WEB NAME:

WEB ADDRESS:

USERNAME:

PASSWORD:

NOTES:

X

WEB NAME:

WEB ADDRESS:

USERNAME:

PASSWORD:

NOTES:

WEB NAME:

WEB ADDRESS:

USERNAME:

PASSWORD:

NOTES:

WEB NAME:

WEB ADDRESS:

USERNAME:

PASSWORD:

NOTES:

X

y

WEB NAME:

WEB ADDRESS:

USERNAME:

PASSWORD:

NOTES:

WEB NAME:

WEB ADDRESS:

USERNAME:

PASSWORD:

NOTES:

WEB NAME:

WEB ADDRESS:

USERNAME:

PASSWORD:

NOTES:

WEB NAME:

WEB ADDRESS:

USERNAME:

PASSWORD:

NOTES:

WEB NAME:

WEB ADDRESS:

USERNAME:

PASSWORD:

NOTES:

WEB NAME:

WEB ADDRESS:

USERNAME:

PASSWORD:

NOTES:

y

WEB NAME:

WEB ADDRESS:

USERNAME:

PASSWORD:

NOTES:

WEB NAME:

WEB ADDRESS:

USERNAME:

PASSWORD:

NOTES:

WEB NAME:

WEB ADDRESS:

USERNAME:

PASSWORD:

NOTES:

WEB NAME:

WEB ADDRESS:

USERNAME:

PASSWORD:

NOTES:

WEB NAME:

WEB ADDRESS:

USERNAME:

PASSWORD:

NOTES:

WEB NAME:

WEB ADDRESS:

USERNAME:

PASSWORD:

NOTES:

y

WEB NAME:

WEB ADDRESS:

USERNAME:

PASSWORD:

NOTES:

WEB NAME:

WEB ADDRESS:

USERNAME:

PASSWORD:

NOTES:

WEB NAME:

WEB ADDRESS:

USERNAME:

PASSWORD:

NOTES:

WEB NAME:

WEB ADDRESS:

USERNAME:

PASSWORD:

NOTES:

WEB NAME:

WEB ADDRESS:

USERNAME:

PASSWORD:

NOTES:

WEB NAME:

WEB ADDRESS:

USERNAME:

PASSWORD:

NOTES:

Z

WEB NAME:

WEB ADDRESS:

USERNAME:

PASSWORD:

NOTES:

WEB NAME:

WEB ADDRESS:

USERNAME:

PASSWORD:

NOTES:

WEB NAME:

WEB ADDRESS:

USERNAME:

PASSWORD:

NOTES:

WEB NAME:

WEB ADDRESS:

USERNAME:

PASSWORD:

NOTES:

WEB NAME:

WEB ADDRESS:

USERNAME:

PASSWORD:

NOTES:

WEB NAME:

WEB ADDRESS:

USERNAME:

PASSWORD:

NOTES:

WEB NAME:

WEB ADDRESS:

Z **USERNAME:**

PASSWORD:

NOTES:

WEB NAME:

WEB ADDRESS:

USERNAME:

PASSWORD:

NOTES:

WEB NAME:

WEB ADDRESS:

USERNAME:

PASSWORD:

NOTES:

WEB NAME:

WEB ADDRESS:

USERNAME:

Z

PASSWORD:

NOTES:

WEB NAME:

WEB ADDRESS:

USERNAME:

PASSWORD:

NOTES:

WEB NAME:

WEB ADDRESS:

USERNAME:

PASSWORD:

NOTES:

Z

WEB NAME:

WEB ADDRESS:

USERNAME:

PASSWORD:

NOTES:

WEB NAME:

WEB ADDRESS:

USERNAME:

PASSWORD:

NOTES:

WEB NAME:

WEB ADDRESS:

USERNAME:

PASSWORD:

NOTES:

WEB NAME:

WEB ADDRESS:

USERNAME:

Z

PASSWORD:

NOTES:

WEB NAME:

WEB ADDRESS:

USERNAME:

PASSWORD:

NOTES:

WEB NAME:

WEB ADDRESS:

USERNAME:

PASSWORD:

NOTES:

NOTES:

NOTES:

NOTES:

NOTES:

NOTES:

NOTES:

NOTES:

NOTES:

NOTES:

NOTES:

NOTES:

NOTES: